The Sirtfood Diet

Step-by-Step Guide For A Quick Weight Loss
And Restoring Health

28-Day Meal Plan

Mell Robinson

CONTENIDO

INTRODUCTION

Want to follow a diet but not sure where to start? Do you find it challenging to find delicious and tummy-filling recipes when going "against the traditional American diet"? Do not worry! This book will provide you with fantastic solutions that will get you started in an instant, but it will also teach you the ultimate tricks for adopting a healthy lifestyle forever.

Mouth-watering delights for any occasion and any eater, you will not believe that these recipes will help you restore your health and slim your body.

What is the Sirtfood Diet?

Successfully adopted by celebrities, the Sirtfood diet has proven to be one of the best lifestyle changes for long-term success for anyone. The restriction list may be frightening at the beginning, but the truth is, this diet is super adaptable, and the food combinations and tasty meals are endless.

Sirtfoods are rich in polyphenols, which are compounds found in some fruits, vegetables, seeds, and cereals. These polyphenols make the sirtuins, a group of proteins that regulate cell health, activate the body's capabilities of burning fat quicker than usual.

Thanks to the polyphenols, our bodies mimic the process of fasting or lower calories consumption, and therefore weight loss occurs. For example, resveratrol, which is found in red grapes and red wine, has an incredible effect on longevity.

No more sluggish afternoons and crunching hunger pangs at midnight. Research shows that resveratrol delays aging and significantly decreases age-related diseases.

Benefits of the Sirtfood diet

These 20 main foods are an excellent source for many nutrients that boost the body's metabolism in so many different ways. They are easy to digest thanks to their rich content of antioxidants, polyphenols, minerals, and vitamins.

- **Lasting Weight-Loss Success and Burning Stomach Fat**
- **Improved Cognitive Incline**
- **Longevity and Improved Memory**

What to eat on the Sirtfood Diet

- **Fruits -** the berries are the way to go - especially strawberries, raspberries, blueberries, and blackberries. Also, Medjool dates stimulate weight loss and are full of polyphenols.

- **Vegetables -** most greeny vegetables are permissible on the sirtfood diet, especially arugula, capers, green chilies, green tea, garlic, celery, parsley, kale, red onion, and red endive.

- **Legumes** are an excellent source of high-quality carbs, protein, and fiber. Fiber is one nutrient that many people lack, and it's essential to boost their consumption.

- **Buckwheat** provides nutrients like selenium, copper, and magnesium to the body. Meanwhile, they are rich in fiber when consumed in their whole forms. Avoid gluten-packed white flour, pasta, and pizza.

- **Walnuts and other healthy nuts -** Nuts are an essential source of selenium, vitamin E, and plant-based protein. They are excellent additions to desserts, smoothies, and snacks. Consume pecans, pistachios, and pine nuts.

- **Seeds** are rich in calcium, vitamins, and healthy fats. Consume chia seeds, hemp seeds, flaxseeds, pumpkin seeds, sunflower seeds, sesame seeds.

- **Extra-Virgin Olive Oil and other healthy oils -** Plants offer some sweet-smelling, healthy oils and fats options perfect for baking, frying, sautéing, etc. They serve as an excellent dairy replacement and are rich in omega-3 fatty acids. Use olive oil or coconut oil.

- **Lean Meat & Plant-Based Foods are excellent for Protein -** Have tofu, tempeh, low-fat chicken, lean red meat, fish, and seafood.

- **Spices, Herbs, and Condiments -** Parsley and Turmeric are amazing, though basil, black pepper, rosemary, oregano, thyme, and sage can be consumed as well.

- **Beverages -** Coffee, water, green tea, red wine and smoothies.

28-DAY MEAL PLAN

PHASE 1 1000 CALORIES

DAY 1

Breakfast, **Snack** & **Dinner**: Power Green Smoothie x3
Lunch: Minty Pesto Rubbed Beef Tenderloins

DAY 2

Breakfast, **Snack** & **Dinner**: Delicious Matcha Smoothie x2
Lunch: Endive & Arugula Tofu Salad with Pesto

DAY 3

Breakfast, **Snack** & **Dinner**: Ginger & Apple Green Smoothie x3
Lunch: Greek-Style Chicken with Olives & Capers

PHASE 2 1500 CALORIES

DAY 4

Breakfast: Morning Matcha Smoothie
Lunch: Sirtfood Frittata
Snack: Energizing Cacao Protein Shake
Dinner: Fried Cod with Celery Wine Sauce

DAY 5

Breakfast: Treacle Buckwheat Granola
Lunch: Vegetable Frittata with Red Onions & Green Chilies
Snack: Chili Toasted Nuts
Dinner: Parsley-Lime Shrimp Pasta

DAY 6

Breakfast: Cinnamon Buckwheat with Walnuts
Lunch: Endive with Cheddar & Walnut Sauce
Snack: Date Cake Slices
Dinner: Fluffy Chocolate Mousse with Strawberries

DAY 7

Breakfast: Strawberry Chocolate Shake
Lunch: Vegetable Frittata with Red Onions & Green Chilies
Snack: Walnut & Chocolate Bars
Dinner: Minty Pesto Rubbed Beef Tenderloins

DAY 8

Breakfast: Power Green Smoothie
Lunch: Hummus & Vegetable Pizza
Snack: Walnut & Chocolate Bars
Dinner: Mixed Grilled Vegetables with Beef Steaks

DAY 9

Breakfast: Cinnamon Buckwheat with Walnuts
Lunch: Endive with Cheddar & Walnut Sauce
Snack: Chili Toasted Nuts
Dinner: Fried Cod with Celery Wine Sauce

DAY 10

Breakfast: Strawberry Chocolate Shake
Lunch: Sirtfood Frittata
Snack: Mini Berry Tarts
Dinner: Crispy Salmon Shirataki Fettucine

DAY 11

Breakfast: Power Green Smoothie
Lunch: Buckwheat Noodles with Cannellini Beans & Tofu
Snack: Delicious Matcha Smoothie
Dinner: Minty Pesto Rubbed Beef Tenderloins

DAY 12

Breakfast: Morning Matcha Smoothie
Lunch: Hummus & Vegetable Pizza
Snack: Delicious Matcha Smoothie
Dinner: Buckwheat Noodles with Cannellini Beans & Tofu

DAY 13

Breakfast: Power Green Smoothie
Lunch: Hummus & Vegetable Pizza
Snack: Date Cake Slices
Dinner: Pesto Arugula Pizza

DAY 14

Breakfast: Morning Matcha Smoothie
Lunch: Buckwheat Noodles with Cannellini Beans & Tofu
Snack: Chili Toasted Nuts
Dinner: Crispy Salmon Shirataki Fettucine

DAY 15

Breakfast: Power Green Smoothie
Lunch: Creole Tempeh & Black Bean Bowls
Snack: Date Cake Slices
Dinner: Parsley-Lime Shrimp Pasta

DAY 16

Breakfast: Morning Matcha Smoothie
Lunch: Vegetable Frittata with Red Onions & Green Chilies
Snack: Strawberry Chocolate Shake
Dinner: Fried Cod with Celery Wine Sauce

DAY 17

Breakfast: Cinnamon Buckwheat with Walnuts
Lunch: Sirtfood Frittata
Snack: Date Cake Slices
Dinner: Mixed Grilled Vegetables with Beef Steaks

PHASE 3 NORMAL AMOUNT OF CALORIES

DAY 18

Breakfast: Power Green Smoothie
Lunch: Buckwheat Noodles with Cannellini Beans & Tofu
Snack: Peanut Butter Blossom Biscuits
Dinner: Fluffy Chocolate Mousse with Strawberries

DAY 19

Breakfast: Strawberry Chocolate Shake
Lunch: Creole Tempeh & Black Bean Bowls
Snack: Chili Toasted Nuts
Dinner: Minty Pesto Rubbed Beef Tenderloins

DAY 20

Breakfast: Power Green Smoothie
Lunch: Endive with Cheddar & Walnut Sauce
Snack: Delicious Matcha Smoothie
Dinner: Italian Chicken Thighs with Soba Noodles

DAY 21

Breakfast: Cinnamon Buckwheat with Walnuts
Lunch: Parsley-Lime Shrimp Pasta
Snack: Nut Stuffed Sweet Apples
Dinner: Crispy Salmon Shirataki Fettucine

DAY 22

Breakfast: Power Green Smoothie
Lunch: Buckwheat Noodles with Cannellini Beans & Tofu
Snack: Nut Stuffed Sweet Apples
Dinner: Fried Cod with Celery Wine Sauce

DAY 23

Breakfast: Morning Matcha Smoothie
Lunch: Buckwheat Noodles with Cannellini Beans & Tofu
Snack: Date Cake Slices
Dinner: Fluffy Chocolate Mousse with Strawberries

DAY 24

Breakfast: Cinnamon Buckwheat with Walnuts
Lunch: Hummus & Vegetable Pizza
Snack: Walnut & Chocolate Bars
Dinner: Mixed Grilled Vegetables with Beef Steaks

DAY 25

Breakfast: Power Green Smoothie
Lunch: Endive with Cheddar & Walnut Sauce
Snack: Walnut & Chocolate Bars
Dinner: Parsley-Lime Shrimp Pasta

DAY 26

Breakfast: Morning Matcha Smoothie
Lunch: Creole Tempeh & Black Bean Bowls
Snack: Strawberry Chocolate Shake
Dinner: Minty Pesto Rubbed Beef Tenderloins

DAY 27

Breakfast: Power Green Smoothie
Lunch: Vegetable Frittata with Red Onions & Green Chilies
Snack: Chili Toasted Nuts
Dinner: Italian Chicken Thighs with Soba Noodles

DAY 28

Breakfast: Cinnamon Buckwheat with Walnuts
Lunch: Buckwheat Noodles with Cannellini Beans & Tofu
Snack: Endive with Cheddar & Walnut Sauce
Dinner: Fluffy Chocolate Mousse with Strawberries

SMOOTHIES & BREAKFAST

Delicious Matcha Smoothie

Prep + Cook Time: 5 minutes | Serves: 1

Ingredients

- 1 apple, chopped
- 1 cup spinach, chopped
- ½ avocado
- ½ cup almond milk
- 1 tsp matcha green tea powder

Directions

Purée everything in a blender until smooth, adding 1 cup water if needed. In a food processor, place the pineapple, mango, spinach, avocado, almond milk, water, and matcha powder. Blitz until smooth. Divide between 4 glasses and serve.

Nutritional Info per serving: Calories 288; Fat: 15g; Total Carbs: 45g; Protein: 4g

Strawberry Chocolate Shake

Prep + Cook Time: 10 minutes | Serves: 1

Ingredients

- 1 cup water
- 1 cup frozen strawberries
- 1 oz baby arugula
- ½ avocado
- ½ tsp vanilla extract
- 1 tbsp cacao powder

Directions

In a food processor, add in all the ingredients and blitz until smooth and creamy. Add ice for a thicker consistency, if desired. Serve immediately!

Nutritional Info per serving: Calories 233; Fat: 7g; Total Carbs: 41g; Protein: 2g

Power Green Smoothie

Prep + Cook Time: 10 minutes | Serves: 2

Ingredients

- 1 little gem lettuce, roughly chopped
- 2 cups almond milk
- 1 cup baby spinach, chopped
- 2 Medjool dates, pitted
- A few ice cubes (optionally)

Directions

In a blender, mix in all the ingredients and pulse until completely smooth. Pour into two glasses and serve immediately.

Nutritional Info per serving: Calories 114; Fat: 4g; Total Carbs: 23g; Protein: 2g

Energizing Cacao Protein Shake

Prep + Cook Time: 10 minutes | Serves: 1

Ingredients

- 1 cup water
- 1 green apple, cored and chopped
- 1 Medjool date, pitted
- 1 tbsp cacao powder
- ½ tbsp cinnamon powder
- 2 tbsp pea protein powder
- 4-5 ice cubes

Directions

In a blender, mix water, apples, date, cacao powder, cinnamon, and protein powder. Blitz until completely smooth.

Add in the ice and pulse again until a thick and smooth texture is obtained. Serve right away!

Nutritional Info per serving: Calories 253; Fat: 3g; Total Carbs: 49g; Protein: 15g

Morning Matcha Smoothie

Prep + Cook Time: 10 minutes | Serves: 1

Ingredients

- 1 cup almond milk
- 1 kiwi
- ½ avocado
- ½ inch fresh ginger, peeled (optional; add to taste)
- 1 handful of fresh baby spinach
- ½ teaspoon matcha powder

Directions

In a blender, mix all ingredients and blitz until smooth. Add some pitted dates for more sweetness, if desired. Serve immediately!

Nutritional Info per serving: Calories 316; Fat: 10g; Total Carbs: 61g; Protein: 8g

Ginger & Apple Green Smoothie

Total Time: 5 minutes | Serves: 2

Ingredients

- 1 cup chopped cucumber
- 1 cup curly endive
- 1 apple, peeled and cored
- 2 tbsp lime juice
- 1 cups soy milk
- ½-inch piece peeled fresh ginger
- 1 tbsp chia seeds
- 1 cup unsweetened coconut yogurt

Directions

Put in a food processor the cucumber, curly endive, apple, lime juice, soy milk, ginger, chia seeds, and coconut yogurt. Blend until smooth. Serve.

Nutritional Info per serving: Calories 165; Fat: 4g; Total Carbs:28g; Protein: 7g

Treacle Buckwheat Granola

Prep + Cook Time: 15 minutes | Serves: 1

Ingredients

- 1 cup buckwheat groats
- ½ cup chopped pecans
- ½ cup shredded coconut
- 1 tbsp chia seeds
- 1 tbsp date sugar
- A pinch of sea salt
- ½ tsp ground cardamon
- ½ cup olive oil
- ½ cup black treacle (or molasses)

Directions

Preheat oven to 320 F. In a bowl, add the buckwheat groats, pecans, shredded coconut, chia seeds, coconut sugar, sea salt, and cardamon. Stir to combine.

In a small saucepan over medium-low heat, warm the oil and black treacle until melted and well combined. Spread the mixture evenly onto a lined baking sheet and bake for 25-30 minutes, stirring halfway through for an even baking.

Nutritional Info per serving: Calories 270; Fat: 8g; Total Carbs: 52g; Protein: 9g

Cinnamon Buckwheat with Walnuts

Ingredients

- 1 cup almond milk
- 1 cup water
- 1 cup buckwheat groats, rinsed
- 1 tsp cinnamon
- ¼ cup chopped walnuts
- 2 tbsp pure date syrup

Directions

Place almond milk, water, and buckwheat in a pot over medium heat and bring to a boil. Lower the heat and simmer covered for 15 minutes. Allow sitting covered for 5 minutes. Mix in the cinnamon, walnuts, and date syrup. Serve warm.

Nutritional Info per serving: Calories 245; Fat: 9g; Total Carbs: 37g; Protein: 7g

SALADS

Very Green Tabbouleh Salad

Prep + Cook Time: 15 minutes | Serves: 2

Ingredients

- 2 cups broccoli florets, chopped
- ½ small red onion
- 4 cherry tomatoes, quartered
- 1 lemon
- 1 extra-virgin olive oil
- ½ bunch parsley, stems removed
- 2 leaves kale, stems removed

Directions

In the food processor, pulse parsley, broccoli, and kale with red onion and lemon juice until thoroughly combined. Combine the broccoli with the remaining ingredients. Drizzle with some olive oil and serve.

Nutritional Info per serving: Calories 115; Fat: 5g; Total Carbs: 8g; Protein: 2g

Walnut Apple Salad with Balsamic Dressing

Prep + Cook Time: 15 minutes | Serves: 2

Ingredients

- 2 cups mixed arugula and red endives
- 1 granny smith apple, chopped
- 1 tbsp red onion, finely chopped
- 2 tbsp pumpkin seeds
- 3-4 radishes, sliced 1 tbsp extra-virgin olive oil
- 1 tbsp balsamic vinegar
- Salt to taste

Directions

In a dry skillet over medium heat, toast the pumpkin seeds for 2-3 minutes, shaking occasionally. Remove and let cool for a few minutes. In a bowl, whisk olive oil, vinegar, and salt. Add in the remaining ingredients, and toss to coat. Serve immediately!

Nutritional Info per serving: Calories 213; Fat: 10g; Total Carbs: 19g; Protein: 5g

Italian Cavolo Nero Salad with Apple Cider Vinaigrette

Prep + Cook Time: 15 minutes | Serves: 2

Ingredients

- 4 oz cavolo nero (kale), stems removed, chopped
- ½ carrot, peeled and shredded
- ½ red onion, diced
- ½ fennel bulb, sliced
- 1 tbsp extra-virgin olive oil
- 1 tbsp apple cider vinegar
- 2 tbsp spicy brown mustard
- 1 tbsp maple syrup
- 1 tbsp ginger paste
- Salt and black pepper to taste

Directions

In a salad bowl, whisk the olive oil, vinegar, mustard, maple syrup, ginger, and a pinch of salt and black pepper. Stir well. Add in cavolo nero and mix with your hands to coat.

Stir in the onions and carrots and top with sliced fennel. Mix well and serve right away.

Nutritional Info per serving: Calories 275; Fat: 15g; Total Carbs: 27g; Protein: 7g

Strawberry & Spinach Salad with Walnut Crunch

Total Time: 20 minutes | Serves: 4

Ingredients

- ¼ cup tahini
- 2 tbsp Dijon mustard
- 3 tbsp maple syrup
- 1 tbsp lemon juice
- ½ cup finely chopped walnuts
- 2 tsp soy sauce
- 1 lb baby spinach
- 1 strawberry, sliced

Directions

Preheat oven to 360 F. Line with parchment paper a baking sheet. In a bowl, mix the tahini, mustard, 2 tbsp maple syrup, lemon juice, and salt. Set aside the dressing.

In another bowl, combine the walnuts, soy sauce, and the remaining maple syrup. Spread evenly on the baking sheet and bake for 5 minutes, shaking once until crunchy. Allow cooling for 3 minutes. Combine the spinach and strawberries in a bowl. Pour over the dressing and toss to coat. Serve garnished with the walnut crunch.

Nutritional Info per serving: Calories 234; Fat: 15g; Total Carbs: 20g; Protein: 8g

Endive & Arugula Tofu Salad with Pesto

Prep + Cook Time: 10 minutes | Serves: 1

Ingredients

- ¼ lb tofu, crumbled
- 3 cherry tomatoes, halved
- 8 kalamata olives
- 2 tbsp pesto sauce
- 2 tbsp extra-virgin olive oil
- 1 oz red endive leaves
- 1 oz arugula
- Salt and black pepper to taste

Directions

On a serving platter, scatter arugula and endive leaves. Drizzle with a bit of olive oil. Arrange the tomato slices on top, scatter the olives and drop pieces of crumbled tofu on the platter. Drizzle the pesto sauce all over, and top with a bit of olive oil to serve.

Nutritional Info per serving: Calories 355; Fat: 25g; Total Carbs: 13g; Protein: 12g

Tuscan Sea Bass with Cucumber & Caper Salad

Prep + Cook Time: 22 minutes | Serves: 2

Ingredients

- 2 steaks skinned sea bass
- 1 cucumber, peeled, seeded, cubed
- Salt and black pepper to taste
- ½ cup black olives, pitted and chopped
- 1 tbsp capers, rinsed
- 1 large tomato, diced
- 2 tbsp red wine vinegar
- 1 red onion, sliced
- 2-3 tbsp olive oil
- ¼ cup basil leaves, thinly sliced

Directions

In a bowl, mix cucumbers, olives, capers, tomatoes, vinegar, red onion, olive oil, and basil. Let sit for the flavors to incorporate. Season fish steaks with salt and pepper; grill them on both sides for 8 minutes in total. Serve the steaks warm over a bed of the salad.

Nutritional Info per serving: Calories 338; Fat: 20g; Total Carbs:13 g; Protein: 25g

Prawn & Arugula Salad with Mayo Dressing

Prep + Cook Time: 15 minutes | Serves: 1

Ingredients

- 1 cup arugula
- 2 tsp low-fat mayonnaise
- 1 tsp garlic powder,
- 1 tbsp extra-virgin olive oil
- 5 oz tiger prawns, peeled and deveined
- 1 tsp Dijon mustard
- Salt and chili pepper to taste
- Juice of 1 lemon

Directions

Mix the mayonnaise, garlic powder, lemon juice, and mustard in a bowl until smooth.

Heat olive oil in a skillet over medium heat, add the prawns, season with salt and chili pepper, and fry in the oil for 3 minutes on each side until prawns are pink; set aside.

Place the arugula in a serving bowl and pour half of the dressing on the top. Toss until mixed, and add the remaining dressing. Divide salad onto plates and top with prawns.

Nutritional Info per serving: Calories 215; Fat: 20g; Total Carbs: 6g; Protein: 8g

Dilled Artichoke Salad with Capers

Prep + Cook Time: 30 minutes | Serves: 1

Ingredients

- 3 oz canned artichokes hearts, halved
- Juice and zest of half lemon
- ¼ cup piquillo peppers, chopped
- ¼ cup olives, pitted and sliced
- ¼ tbsp dill, chopped
- Salt and black pepper to taste
- 1 tbsp capers

Directions

Combine all the ingredients, except for the artichokes and olives, in a bowl. Drain and place the artichokes on a serving plate. Pour the prepared mixture over; toss to combine well. Serve topped with the olives.

Nutritional Info per serving: Calories 170; Fat: 13g; Total Carbs: 15g; Protein: 1g

Cherry Tomato & Buckwheat Salad

Prep + Cook Time: 15 minutes | Serves: 2

Ingredients

- ½ cup buckwheat, cooked
- ½ ripe avocado, sliced
- ½ green pepper, cut into chunks
- Salt and black pepper to taste
- ½ cucumber, cut into chunks
- 1 tbsp extra-virgin olive oil
- 4 cherry tomatoes, halved
- 1 tbsp fresh parsley, finely chopped

Directions

Place all vegetables in a bowl and season to taste. Drizzle with olive oil and sprinkle with freshly chopped parsley; stir well and add the buckwheat. Mix well and serve.

Nutritional Info per serving: Calories 353; Fat: 9g; Total Carbs: 62g; Protein: 12g

Tofu Caprese Salad with Pesto & Anchovies

Prep + Cook Time: 15 minutes | Serves: 2

Ingredients

- 2 large red tomatoes, cut into 3 slices
- 12 (1-inch each) fresh Tofu slices
- 2 large yellow tomatoes, cut into 3 slices
- 1 cup basil pesto, olive oil-based
- 4 anchovy fillets in oil

Directions

On a serving platter, alternately stack one red tomato slice, one tofu slice, one yellow tomato, one tofu slice, one red tomato slice, and then one tofu. Repeat making 3 more stacks in the same manner.

Spoon the pesto all over the snacks making sure that they are well-covered with the pesto. Arrange the anchovy fillets on top and serve immediately.

Nutritional Info per serving: Calories 178; Fat: 10g; Total Carbs: 5g; Protein: 17g

Tofu Balls with Spring Salad

Prep + Cook Time: 20 minutes | Serves: 4

Ingredients

For the Tofu Balls:

- 3 eggs
- ½ cups tofu cheese, crumbled
- 1 cup flour
- 1 tbsp flax meal
- 1 tsp baking powder
- Salt and black pepper to taste

For the Salad:

- 1 head red endive
- ½ cup cucumber, thinly sliced
- 2 tomatoes, seeded and chopped
- ½ red onion, thinly sliced
- 10 radishes, thinly sliced
- ⅓ cup low-fat mayonnaise
- 1 tsp Dijon mustard
- Salt to taste

Directions

Line a piece of parchment paper to a baking sheet. In a mixing dish, mix all ingredients for the cheese balls; form balls out of the mixture. Set the balls on the prepared baking sheet. Bake for 10 minutes at 390 F until crisp. Arrange endives leaves on a large salad platter; add in radishes, tomatoes, cucumbers, and red onion.

In a small mixing bowl, mix the mayonnaise, salt, and mustard. Sprinkle this mixture over the vegetables. Add cheese balls on top and serve.

Nutritional Info per serving: Calories 234; Fat: 17g; Total Carbs:18 g; Protein: 12g

SOUPS

Arugula & Green Beans Coconut Soup

Total Time: 30 minutes | Serves: 2

Ingredients

- 1 tsp coconut oil
- 1 red onion, diced
- 1 cup green beans
- 2 cups water
- 1 cup arugula, chopped
- 1 tbsp fresh mint, chopped
- Sea salt and black pepper to taste
- ¾ cup coconut milk

Directions

Place a pot over medium heat and heat the coconut oil. Add in the onion and sauté for 5 minutes. Pour in green beans and water. Bring to a boil, lower the heat and stir in arugula, mint, salt, and pepper. Simmer for 10 minutes. Stir in coconut milk. Transfer to a food processor and blitz the soup until smooth. Serve.

Nutritional Info per serving: Calories 277; Fat: 23g; Total Carbs: 15g; Protein: 4g

Easy Green Soup

Prep + Cook Time: 25 minutes | Serves: 2

Ingredients

- 5 oz broccoli head, chopped
- 1 cup kale, chopped
- ½ red onion, chopped
- 1 garlic cloves, minced
- 1 ½ cups vegetable stock
- ½ cup coconut milk
- 2 tbsp olive oil
- Salt and black pepper to taste
- 2 tbsp fresh parsley, chopped

Directions

Warm olive oil in a large pot over medium heat. Add onion and garlic, and stir-fry for 2-3 minutes until tender. Add broccoli and cook for an additional 10 minutes.

Pour the stock over and bring to a boil; reduce the heat. Simmer for about 3 minutes.

In the end, add kale and cook for 3 more minutes. Stir in the milk, salt, and pepper.

Blend the soup with a hand blender. Serve drizzled with a tbsp of olive oil and scatter fresh parsley to serve.

Nutritional Info per serving: Calories 392; Fat: 17g; Total Carbs: 23g; Protein: 8g

Homemade Ramen Soup

Total Time: 25 minutes | Serves: 2

Ingredients

- 4 oz Japanese buckwheat noodles
- 2 tbsp sesame paste
- 1 cup canned pinto beans, drained
- 2 tbsp fresh parsley, chopped
- 2 scallions, thinly sliced

Directions

In boiling salted water, add in the noodles and cook for 5 minutes over low heat.

Remove a cup of the noodle water to a bowl and add in the sesame paste; stir until it has dissolved.

Pour the sesame mix in the pot with the noodles, add in pinto beans, and stir until everything is hot. Serve topped with parsley and scallions in individual bowls.

Nutritional Info per serving: Calories 504; Fat: 10g; Total Carbs: 78g; Protein: 25g

Spicy Kale & Cauliflower Soup

Prep + Cook Time: 15 minutes | Serves: 2

Ingredients

- 2 tbsp olive oil
- ½ red onion, chopped
- 1 garlic clove, minced
- 1 head cauliflower, cut into florets
- 4 oz kale, chopped
- 2 cups vegetable broth
- ½ cup coconut milk
- Salt to taste
- ½ tsp red pepper flakes
- 1 tbsp fresh parsley, chopped

Directions

Warm the olive oil in a pot over medium-high heat. Add garlic and onion and sauté until browned and softened, about 3 minutes.

Pour in the broth, kale, and cauliflower; cook for 8-10 minutes until the mixture boils. Stir in the salt, pepper, and milk and simmer the soup while covered for 5 minutes.

Transfer the soup to an immersion blender and pulse to achieve desired consistency; top with parsley and serve.

Nutritional Info per serving: Calories 242; Fat: 13g; Total Carbs: 28g; Protein: 12g

Mushroom & Tofu Soup

Total Time: 20 minutes | Serves: 2

Ingredients

- 2 cups water
- 1 tbsp soy sauce
- 2 white mushrooms, sliced
- ¼ cup chopped green onions
- 3 tbsp tahini
- 3 oz extra-firm tofu, diced

Directions

Pour the water and soy sauce into a pot and bring to a boil. Add in mushrooms and green onions. Lower the heat and simmer for 10 minutes.

In a bowl, combine ½ cup of hot soup with tahini. Pour the mixture into the pot and simmer 2 minutes more, but not boil. Stir in tofu. Serve warm.

Nutritional Info per serving: Calories 263; Fat: 20g; Total Carbs: 12g; Protein: 12g

Asian Ginger Broccoli Soup

Total Time: 50 minutes | Serves: 2

Ingredients

- ½ red onion, chopped
- 1 tbsp minced peeled fresh ginger
- 2 tsp olive oil
- 1 carrot, chopped
- ½ head broccoli, chopped into florets
- ½ cup coconut milk
- 1½ cups vegetable broth
- ½ tsp turmeric
- Salt and black pepper to taste

Directions

In a pot over medium heat, place the onion, ginger, and olive oil, cook for 4 minutes. Add in carrots, broccoli, broth, turmeric, pepper, and salt.

Bring to a boil and cook for 15 minutes. Transfer the soup to a food processor and blend until smooth. Stir in coconut milk and serve warm.

Nutritional Info per serving: Calories 226; Fat: 19g; Total Carbs: 15g; Protein: 3g

Effortless Miso Soup

Prep + Cook Time: 25 minutes | Serves: 2

Ingredients

- 2 baby carrots, chopped
- 3 oz cremini mushrooms, sliced
- 2 cups vegetable broth
- 1 tbsp soy sauce
- 1 cup baby spinach leaves
- 2 tbsp red miso paste
- 1 tbsp toasted sesame oil
- 1 tbsp freshly grated ginger
- 1 tbsp extra-virgin olive oil
- ½ cup red onions, chopped

Directions

In a small bowl, mix together miso, sesame oil, and ginger. Set it aside.

Heat the olive oil in a pot over high heat and add in the onions, mushrooms, and carrots. Stir-fry for 5 minutes, until softened. Pour in the broth and bring to a boil.

Reduce the heat and simmer for 10 minutes, partially covered. Remove from the heat and stir in the spinach. Let sit covered until the spinach is wilted, about 5 minutes.

With a ladle, take one scoop (about half a cup) of broth out and add to the miso bowl. Stir until dissolved, then transfer the miso to the pot. Season to taste and serve warm, drizzled with soy sauce!

Nutritional Info per serving: Calories 145; Fat: 10g; Total Carbs: 15g; Protein: 6g

MAIN DISHES

Mediterranean Chicken Breasts

Prep + Cook Time: 65 minutes | Serves: 2

Ingredients

- 2 tsp olive oil
- 1 medium lemon, sliced
- ½ lb chicken breasts, halved
- Salt and black pepper to season
- 1 tbsp capers, rinsed
- 1 cup chicken broth
- 2 tbsp chopped fresh parsley, divided

Directions

Lay a piece of parchment paper on a baking sheet. Preheat the oven to 350ºF.

Lay the lemon slices on the baking sheet, drizzle them with olive oil and sprinkle with salt. Roast in the oven for 25 minutes to brown the lemon rinds.

Cover the chicken with plastic wrap, place them on a flat surface, and gently pound with the rolling pin to flatten to about ½ -inch thickness.

Remove the plastic wraps and season the chicken with salt and pepper; set aside.

Heat the olive oil in a skillet over medium heat and fry the chicken on both sides to a golden brown for about 8 minutes in total.

Then, pour the chicken broth in, shake the skillet, and let the broth boil and reduce to a thick consistency, about 12 minutes.

Lightly stir in capers, roasted lemon, black pepper, olive oil, and parsley; simmer on low heat for 10 minutes. Serve the chicken with the sauce and sprinkled with fresh parsley.

Nutritional Info per serving: Calories 430; Fat: 23g; Total Carbs: 13g; Protein: 33g

Greek-Style Chicken with Olives & Capers

Prep + Cook Time: 30 minutes | Serves: 2

Ingredients

- 2 tbsp olive oil
- 1 red onion, chopped
- ½ lb chicken breasts, skinless and boneless
- 2 garlic cloves, minced
- Salt and black pepper to taste
- ½ cup Kalamata olives, pitted and chopped
- 1 tbsp capers
- 2 tomatoes, chopped
- ½ tsp red chili flakes

Directions

Warm olive oil in a skillet over medium heat and cook the chicken for 2 minutes per side. Sprinkle with black pepper and salt. Set the chicken breasts in the oven at 450ºF and bake for 8 minutes. Arrange the chicken on a platter.

In the same pan over medium heat, add the onion, olives, capers, garlic, and chili flakes, and cook for 1 minute. Stir in the tomatoes, pepper, and salt, and cook for 2 minutes. Sprinkle over the chicken breasts and enjoy.

Nutritional Info per serving: Calories 387; Fat: 21g; Total Carbs: 12g; Protein: 23g

Fried Cod with Celery Wine Sauce

Prep + Cook Time: 20 minutes | Serves: 2

Ingredients

- 2 tsp extra-virgin olive oil
- 2 cod fillets
- 2 garlic cloves, minced
- Juice of 1 lemon
- 3 tbsp white wine
- 1 stalk celery, chopped
- 1 small red onion, chopped
- Salt and black pepper to taste

Directions

Heat 2 tbsp of the oil in a skillet over medium heat and season the cod with salt and black pepper. Fry the fillets in the oil for 4 minutes on one side, flip and cook for 1 minute. Take out, plate, and set aside.

In another skillet over low heat, warm the remaining olive oil and sauté the garlic and celery for 3 minutes. Add the lemon juice, wine, and red onions. Season with salt, black pepper, and cook for 3 minutes until the wine slightly reduces.

Put the fish in the skillet, spoon sauce over, cook for 30 seconds, and turn the heat off. Divide fish into plates, top with sauce, and serve.

Nutritional Info per serving: Calories 264; Fat: 17g; Total Carbs: 9g; Protein: 20g

Minty Pesto Rubbed Beef Tenderloins

Prep + Cook Time: 3 hours 10 minutes | Serves: 1

Ingredients

- 1 cup fresh parsley, roughly chopped
- 1 tsp fresh mint
- 1 red onion, chopped
- 5 oz beef tenderloin
- 1 lemon zested and juiced
- 3 tbsp olive oil, divided
- 1 oz walnuts, chopped
- Salt to taste
- 3 garlic cloves, minced

Directions

Preheat oven to 360 F.

In a food processor, combine the parsley with 2 tbsp of olive oil, mint, garlic, walnuts, salt, lemon zest, and red onion. Rub the beef with the mixture, place in a bowl, and refrigerate for 1 hour covered.

Remove the beef and warm 1 tbsp of olive oil in a skillet over high heat. Sear the meat for 3 to 5 minutes, depending on how you like it done. Transfer to a baking dish and cook in the oven for 16 minutes. Serve with a salad.

Nutritional Info per serving: Calories 528; Fat: 38g; Total Carbs: 23g; Protein: 37g

Crispy Salmon Shirataki Fettucine

Prep + Cook Time: 35 minutes | Serves: 2

Ingredients

For the shirataki fettuccine:

- 1 (4 oz) pack shirataki fettuccine

For the creamy salmon sauce:

- 3 tbsp extra-virgin olive oil
- 2 salmon fillets, cut into 2-inch cubes
- Salt and black pepper to taste
- 3 garlic cloves, minced
- 1 cup heavy cream
- ½ cup dry white wine
- 1 tsp grated lemon zest
- 1 cup baby spinach
- Lemon wedges for garnishing

Directions

For the shirataki fettuccine:

Boil 2 cups of water in a pot over medium heat. Strain the shirataki pasta through a colander and rinse very well under hot running water. Pour the shirataki pasta into the boiling water. Take off the heat, let sit for 3 minutes and strain again.

Place a dry skillet over medium heat and stir-fry the shirataki pasta until visibly dry, and makes a squeaky sound when stirred, 1 to 2 minutes. Take off the heat and set aside.

For the salmon sauce:

Melt half of the olive oil in a large skillet; season the salmon with salt, black pepper, and cook in the butter until golden brown on all sides and flaky within, 8 minutes. Transfer to a plate and set aside. Add the remaining olive oil to the skillet and stir in the garlic. Cook until fragrant, 1 minute.

Mix in heavy cream, white wine, lemon zest, salt, and pepper. Allow boiling over low heat for 5 minutes. Stir in spinach, allow wilting for 2 minutes and stir in shirataki fettuccine and salmon until well-coated in the sauce. Garnish with the lemon wedges.

Nutritional Info per serving: Calories 773; Fat: 48g; Total Carbs: 21g; Protein: 65g

Italian Chicken Thighs with Soba Noodles

Total Time: 30 minutes + overnight chilling time| Serves: 4

Ingredients

- 16 oz buckwheat noodles
- 3 tbsp extra-virgin olive oil
- 4 chicken thighs, cut into 1-inch pieces
- Salt and black pepper to taste
- 1 red onion, chopped
- 4 garlic cloves, minced
- 1 cup cherry tomatoes, halved
- ½ cup chicken broth
- 2 cups baby kale, chopped
- 1 cup grated Parmesan cheese for serving
- 2 tbsp capers for topping

Directions

Cook buckwheat noodles according to package instructions; set aside.

Heat the olive oil in a medium pot, season the chicken with salt, black pepper, and sear in the oil until golden brown on the outside. Transfer to a plate and set aside.

Add the onion and garlic to the oil and cook until softened and fragrant, 3 minutes.

Mix in the tomatoes and chicken broth, cover, and cook over low heat until the tomatoes soften, and the liquid reduces by half. Season with salt and black pepper.

Return the chicken to the pot and stir in the kale. Wilt for 2 minutes.

Share the noodles onto serving plates, top with the kale sauce, and then the Parmesan cheese. Garnish with capers and serve warm.

Nutritional Info per serving: Calories 578; Fat: 39g; Total Carbs: 36g; Protein: 27g

Parsley-Lime Shrimp Pasta

Prep + Cook Time: 20 minutes | Serves: 4

Ingredients

- 2 tbsp butter
- 1 lb jumbo shrimp, peeled and deveined
- 4 garlic cloves, minced
- 1 pinch red chili flakes
- ¼ cup white wine
- 1 lime, zested and juiced
- 3 medium zucchinis, spiralized
- Salt and black pepper to taste
- 2 tbsp chopped parsley
- 1 cup grated Parmesan cheese for topping

Directions

Melt the butter in a large skillet and cook the shrimp until starting to turn pink.

Flip and stir in the garlic and red chili flakes. Cook further for 1 minute or until the shrimp is pink and opaque. Transfer to a plate and set aside.

Pour the wine and lime juice into the skillet, and cook until reduced by a quarter. Meanwhile, stir to deglaze the bottom of the pot.

Mix in the zucchinis, lime zest, shrimp, and parsley. Season with salt and black pepper, and toss everything well. Cook until the zucchinis is slightly tender for 2 minutes. Dish the food onto serving plates and top generously with the Parmesan cheese.

Nutritional Info per serving: Calories 315; Fat: 10g; Total Carbs: 43g; Protein: 27g

Mixed Grilled Vegetables with Beef Steaks

Prep + Cook Time: 30 minutes | Serves: 2

Ingredients

- ½ pound sirloin steaks
- 2 tbsp olive oil
- Salt and black pepper to taste
- 2 tbsp balsamic vinegar

Vegetables

- 4 asparagus, trimmed
- 1 red onion, quartered
- 2 oz kale
- 2 green chili peppers, cut into strips

Directions

Grab 2 separate bowls; put the beef in one and the vegetables in another. Mix salt, pepper, olive oil, and balsamic vinegar in a small bowl, and pour half of the mixture over the beef and the other half over the vegetables. Coat the ingredients in both bowls with the sauce.

Preheat grill to high. Place the steaks and sear for 4 minutes, then flip, and continue cooking for 6 minutes. When done, remove the beef to a plate; set aside.

Pour the vegetables and marinade in the same grill pan, and cook for 5 minutes, turning once. Turn the heat off and share the vegetables into four plates. Top with each piece of beef, the sauce from the pan, and serve.

Nutritional Info per serving: Calories 417; Fat: 25g; Total Carbs: 18g; Protein: 27g

Creamy Mussels with Soba Noodles

Prep + Cook Time: 25 minutes | Serves: 4

Ingredients

- 8 oz Soba buckwheat noodles
- 1 lb mussels, debearded and rinsed
- 1 cup white wine
- 4 tbsp extra-virgin olive oil
- 1 large red onion, finely chopped
- 6 garlic cloves, minced
- 2 tsp red chili flakes
- ½ cup fish stock
- 1 ½ cups heavy cream
- 2 tbsp chopped fresh parsley
- Salt and black pepper to taste

Directions

Cook buckwheat noodles according to package instructions; set aside.

Pour mussels and white wine into a pot, cover, and cook for 4 minutes. Occasionally stir until the mussels have opened. Strain the mussels and reserve the cooking liquid. Allow cooling, discard any mussels with closed shells, and remove the meat out of ¾ of the mussel shells. Set aside with the remaining mussels in the shells.

Heat olive oil in a skillet and sauté shallots, garlic, and chili flakes for 3 minutes. Mix in reduced wine and fish stock. Allow boiling and whisk in the remaining butter and then the heavy cream. Taste the sauce and adjust the taste with salt, pepper, and mix in parsley. Pour in the shirataki pasta, mussels and toss well in the sauce. Serve afterward.

Nutritional Info per serving: Calories 431; Fat: 28g; Total Carbs: 49g; Protein: 18g

VEGETARIAN AND VEGAN MAIN DISHES

Creole Tofu Scramble with Kale

Prep + Cook Time: 40 minutes | Serves: 2

Ingredients

- 2 tbsp extra-virgin olive oil, for frying
- 1 (14 oz) pack firm tofu, pressed and crumbled
- 4 green chilies, deseeded and chopped
- 1 tomato, finely chopped
- 2 tbsp chopped fresh green onions
- Salt and black pepper to taste
- 1 tsp turmeric powder
- 1 tsp Creole seasoning
- ½ cup chopped baby kale
- ¼ cup grated Parmesan cheese

Directions

Heat the olive oil in a large skillet over medium heat and cook the tofu with occasional stirring until light golden brown. Make sure not to break the tofu into tiny bits but to have scrambled egg resemblance, 5 minutes.

Stir in the chilies, tomato, green onions, salt, black pepper, turmeric powder, and Creole seasoning. Sauté until the vegetables soften, 5 minutes.

Mix in the kale to wilt, 3 minutes, and then half of Parmesan cheese. Melt for 2 minutes and turn the heat off. Dish the food, top with the remaining cheese, and serve warm.

Nutritional Info per serving: Calories 258; Fat: 16g; Total Carbs: 14g; Protein: 21g

Vegetable Frittata with Red Onions & Green Chilies

Prep + Cook Time: 25 minutes | Serves: 1

Ingredients

- 1 tbsp extra-virgin olive oil
- ½ small red onion, chopped
- 1 green chili pepper, chopped
- ½ carrot, chopped
- ½ zucchini, chopped
- 1 tsp turmeric
- 3 eggs
- Salt and black pepper to taste
- 1 tbsp fresh parsley, chopped

Directions

Preheat the oven to 350ºF.

Warm olive oil in a pan over medium heat. Stir in red onions and sauté for 3 minutes until tender. Pour in carrot, zucchini, and green chili, and cook for 4 minutes. Remove the mixture to a greased baking pan with cooking spray.

In a bowl, whisk the eggs with turmeric, salt, and pepper and pour over vegetables. Bake for 10-15 minutes until golden. Drizzle with freshly chopped parsley and serve.

Nutritional Info per serving: Calories 288; Fat: 23g; Total Carbs: 11g; Protein: 13g

Sirtfood Frittata

Prep + Cook Time: 15 minutes | Serves: 2

Ingredients

- 2 tsp olive oil
- 1 small red onion, chopped
- 2 garlic cloves, chopped
- 4 eggs, beaten
- 2 tomatoes, sliced
- 1 green chili, minced
- 2 tbsp fresh parsley, chopped
- Salt and black pepper, to taste

Directions

Set a pan over high heat and warm the olive oil. Sauté garlic and red onion until tender.

Whisk the eggs with yogurt. Pour into the pan and cook until eggs become puffy and brown to bottom. Add parsley, chili pepper and tomatoes to one side of the omelet. Season with black pepper and salt. Fold the omelet in half and slice into wedges.

Nutritional Info per serving: Calories 319; Fat: 25g; Total Carbs: 20g; Protein: 14g

Baby Arugula Stuffed Zucchini

Prep + Cook Time: 40 minutes | Serves: 2

Ingredients

- 2 zucchinis, halved
- 4 tbsp olive oil
- 2 garlic cloves, minced
- 1½ oz baby arugula
- Salt and black pepper to taste
- 2 tbsp tomato sauce
- 1 cup Parmesan cheese, shredded

Directions

Scoop out the pulp of the zucchinis into a plate. Keep the flesh. Grease a baking sheet with cooking spray and place in the zucchini halves.

Warm the olive oil in a skillet over medium heat. Sauté the garlic until fragrant, about 1 minute. Add arugula and zucchini pulp. Cook until the arugula wilts; season with salt and pepper. Spoon the tomato sauce into the boats and spread to coat the bottom.

Spoon the arugula mixture into the zucchinis and sprinkle with the vegan parmesan cheese. Bake in the oven for 20 to 25 minutes at 370ºF or until the cheese has a beautiful golden color. Plate the zucchinis when ready, season with salt and black pepper. .

Nutritional Info per serving: Calories 520; Fat: 37g; Total Carbs: 19g; Protein: 20g

Celery Buckwheat Croquettes

Total Time: 25 minutes | Serves: 2

Ingredients

- ¾ cup buckwheat groats, cooked
- 3 tbsp extra-virgin olive oil
- ¼ cup minced red onion
- 1 celery stalk, chopped
- ¼ cup shredded carrots
- 1/3 cup buckwheat flour
- ¼ cup chopped fresh parsley
- Salt and black pepper to taste

Directions

Place the groats in a bowl. Heat 1 tbsp of oil in a skillet over medium heat. Place in onion, celery, and carrot and stir-fry for 5 minutes. Transfer to the buckwheat bowl.

Mix in flour, parsley, salt, and pepper. Place in the fridge for 20 minutes. Mold the mixture into cylinder-shaped balls. Heat the remaining oil in a skillet over medium heat. Fry the croquettes for 8 minutes, turning occasionally until golden.

Nutritional Info per serving: Calories 230; Fat: 10g; Total Carbs: 32g; Protein: 6g

Creole Tempeh & Black Bean Bowls

Prep + Cook Time: 50 minutes | Serves: 4

Ingredients

- 2 tbsp olive oil
- 1 ½ cups crumbled tempeh
- 1 tsp Creole seasoning
- 2 red bell peppers, deseeded and sliced
- 2 cups vegetable broth
- Salt to taste
- 1 (8 oz) can black beans, drained and rinsed
- 2 chives, chopped
- 2 tbsp freshly chopped parsley

Directions

Heat the olive oil in a medium pot and cook in the tempeh until golden brown, 5 minutes. Season with the Creole seasoning and stir in the bell peppers. Cook until the peppers slightly soften, 3 minutes.

Stir in the beans, vegetable broth, and salt. Cover and cook until the liquid is absorbed, 5 to 10 minutes. Stir in the chives and dish the food, garnished with the parsley.

Nutritional Info per serving: Calories 216; Fat: 18g; Total Carbs: 15g; Protein: 21g

Spicy Broccoli Pasta

Prep + Cook Time: 20 minutes | Serves: 2

Ingredients

- 5 oz buckwheat fusilli
- 4 oz broccoli florets
- 1 tbsp extra-virgin olive oil
- 1 small red onion, finely sliced
- 1 garlic clove, finely sliced
- ½ tsp crushed chilies
- ½ tsp caraway seeds
- 1 large zucchini, coarsely grated
- 4 tbsp low-fat heavy milk
- ½ lemon, zested and juiced
- 3-4 ice cubes

Directions

Prepare the pasta according to package instructions. 4 minutes before the end, add in the broccoli to the pan. Drain and keep 3 tbsp of the pasta water.

In the meantime, warm the oil in a large skillet over a low heat. Add the onion and cook for 5 mins, then stir in the garlic, crushed chilies and caraway seeds. Cook 4-5 minutes more. Add the zucchini and season to taste. Fry until the zucchini is tender, 2 minutes..

Add the pasta, broccoli and reserved pasta water to the skillet. Remove from the heat and stir in the heavy cream and lemon juice. Serve warm.

Nutritional Info per serving: Calories 304; Fat: 10g; Total Carbs: 39g; Protein: 11g

Buckwheat Pilaf with Pine Nuts

Total Time: 25 minutes | Serves: 2

Ingredients

- 1 cup buckwheat groats
- 2 cups vegetable stock
- ¼ cup walnuts
- 2 tbsp olive oil
- ½ red onion, chopped
- ⅓ cup chopped fresh parsley

Directions

Put the groats and vegetable stock in a pot. Bring to a boil, then lower the heat and simmer for 15 minutes. Heat a skillet over medium heat. Place in the pine nuts and toast for 2-3 minutes, shaking often. Heat the oil in the same skillet and sauté the onion for 3 minutes until translucent.

Once the groats are ready, fluff them using a fork. Mix in walnuts, onion, and parsley. Sprinkle with salt and pepper. Serve.

Nutritional Info per serving: Calories 277; Fat: 19g; Total Carbs: 21g; Protein: 5g

Buckwheat Savoy Cabbage Rolls with Tofu

Prep + Cook Time: 30 minutes | Serves: 2

Ingredients

- 2 tbsp extra-virgin olive oil
- 2 cups extra firm tofu, pressed and crumbled
- ½ medium red onion, finely chopped
- 2 garlic cloves, minced
- Salt and black pepper to taste
- 1 cup buckwheat groats
- 1 ¾ cups vegetable stock
- 1 bay leaf
- 2 tbsp chopped fresh cilantro + more for garnishing
- 1 head Savoy cabbage, leaves separated (scraps kept)
- 1 (23 oz) canned chopped tomatoes

Directions

Warm the olive oil in a large skillet and cook the tofu until golden brown, 8 minutes. Stir in the onion and garlic until softened and fragrant, 3 minutes. Season with salt, black pepper and mix in the buckwheat, bay leaf, and vegetable stock.

Close the lid, allow boiling, and then simmer until all the liquid is absorbed. Open the lid; remove the bay leaf, adjust the taste with salt, black pepper, and mix in the cilantro.

Lay the cabbage leaves on a flat surface and add 3 to 4 tablespoons of the cooked buckwheat onto each leaf. Roll the leaves to firmly secure the filling.

Pour the tomatoes with juices into a medium pot, season with a little salt, black pepper, and lay the cabbage rolls in the sauce. Cook over medium heat until the cabbage softens, 5 to 8 minutes. Turn the heat off and dish the food onto serving plates. Garnish with more cilantro and serve warm.

Nutritional Info per serving: Calories 598; Fat: 28g; Total Carbs: 53g; Protein: 48g

Buckwheat Noodles with Cannellini Beans & Tofu

Prep + Cook Time: 35 minutes | Serves: 2

Ingredients

- 8 oz buckwheat noodles (Soba)
- 1 tbsp olive oil
- 1 medium zucchini, sliced
- 2 garlic cloves, minced
- 2 large tomatoes, chopped
- 1 (15 oz) can cannellini beans, rinsed and drained
- 1 (2 ¼ oz) can pitted green olives, sliced
- ½ cup crumbled tofu cheese

Directions

Cook the noodles in salted water in a medium pot over until al dente, 4-6 minutes. Drain and set aside.

Heat olive oil in a skillet and sauté zucchini and garlic for 4 minutes. Stir in tomatoes, beans, and olives. Cook until the tomatoes soften, 10 minutes. Mix in pasta, and warm through for 1 minute. Stir in crumbled tofu nd serve.

Nutritional Info per serving: Calories 206; Fat: 12g; Total Carbs: 37g; Protein: 12g

Hummus & Vegetable Pizza

Prep + Cook Time: 30 minutes | Serves: 2

Ingredients

For the pizza crust:
- 1 cup buckwheat flour
- 1 cup white wheat flour
- 1 tsp yeast
- 1 tsp salt
- 1 pinch brown sugar
- 3 tbsp olive oil
- 1 ½ cups warm water

For the topping:
- 1 cup hummus
- 8 cremini mushrooms, sliced
- ½ cup fresh baby spinach
- ½ cup cherry tomatoes, halved
- ½ cup sliced Kalamata olives
- ½ red onion, sliced
- 1 tsp dried oregano

Directions

Preheat the oven the 350 F and lightly grease a pizza pan with cooking spray. In a medium bowl, mix the flours, nutritional yeast, salt, sugar, olive oil, and warm water until smooth dough forms. Allow rising for an hour or until the dough doubles in size.

Spread the dough on the pizza pan and spread the hummus on the dough. Add the mushrooms, spinach, tomatoes, olives, red onion, and top with the oregano. Bake the pizza for 20 minutes or until the mushrooms soften. Remove from the oven, cool for 5 minutes, slice, and serve.

Nutritional Info per serving: Calories 592; Fat: 20g; Total Carbs: 93g; Protein: 18g

Portobello Kale Florentine with Tofu

Prep + Cook Time: 25 minutes | Serves: 2

Ingredients

- 4 large portobello mushrooms, stems removed
- 1/8 tsp black pepper
- 1/8 tsp garlic salt
- ½ tsp olive oil
- 1 small red onion, chopped
- 1 cup chopped fresh kale
- ¼ cup crumbled Tofu
- 1 tbsp chopped fresh parsley

Directions

Preheat the oven to 350 F and grease a baking sheet with cooking spray.

Lightly oil the mushrooms with some cooking spray and season with the black pepper and garlic salt. Arrange the mushrooms on the baking sheet and bake in the oven until tender, 10 to 15 minutes.

Heat the olive oil in a medium skillet over medium heat and sauté the onion until tender, 3 minutes. Stir in the kale until wilted, 3 minutes. Turn the heat off. Spoon the mixture into the mushrooms and top with the tofu and parsley. Serve.

Nutritional Info per serving: Calories 185; Fat: 8g; Total Carbs: 23g; Protein: 10g

Pesto Arugula Pizza

Total Time: 30 minutes | Serves: 4

Ingredients

For the crust:

- ½ cup almond flour
- ¼ tsp salt
- 2 tbsp ground psyllium husk
- 1 tbsp olive oil
- 1 cup lukewarm water

For the topping:

- 1 cup basil pesto, olive oil-based
- 1 cup goat cheese, crumbled
- 1 tomato, thinly sliced
- 1 green chilies, sliced
- 1 cup baby arugula
- 2 tbsp chopped walnuts
- ¼ tsp red chili flakes

Directions

Preheat the oven to 425 F and line a baking sheet with parchment paper.

In a medium bowl, mix the almond flour, salt, psyllium powder, olive oil, and lukewarm water until dough forms.

Spread the mixture on the pizza pan and bake in the oven until crusty, 10 minutes.

When ready, remove the crust and allow cooling. Spread the pesto on the crust and top with the goat cheese, tomato, and green chilies.

Bake in the oven until the cheese melts, 15 minutes. Remove the pizza from the oven; top with the arugula, walnuts, and red chili flakes. Slice and serve the pizza warm.

Nutritional Info per serving: Calories 386; Fat: 24g; Total Carbs: 54g; Protein: 15g

Zucchini Rolls in Tomato Sauce

Prep + Cook Time: 20 minutes | Serves: 2

Ingredients

- 3 large zucchinis, sliced lengthwise into strips
- Salt and black pepper to taste
- 1 cup crumbled tofu
- 1/3 cup grated Parmesan cheese
- ¼ cup chopped fresh basil leaves
- 2 garlic cloves, minced
- 1 ½ cups marinara sauce, divided
- ½ cup shredded mozzarella, divided

Directions

Line a baking sheet with paper towels and lay the zucchini slices in a single layer on the sheet. Sprinkle each side with some salt and allow releasing of liquid for 15 minutes.

In a medium bowl, mix the tofu, Parmesan cheese, basil and garlic; season with salt and black pepper. Preheat the oven to 400 F.

Spread 1 cup of marinara sauce onto the bottom of a 10-inch oven-proof skillet and set aside. Spread 1 tbsp of the tofu/Parmesan mixture evenly along each zucchini slice; sprinkle with 1 tbsp of mozzarella cheese.

Roll up the zucchini slices over the filling and arrange in the skillet. Top with the remaining ½ cup of marinara sauce and sprinkle with the remaining mozzarella.

Bake in the oven for 25-30 minutes or until the zucchini rolls are heated through and the cheese begins to brown. Serve immediately.

Nutritional Info per serving: Calories 328; Fat: 17g; Total Carbs: 32g; Protein: 21g

Buckwheat Puttanesca with Olives & Capers

Prep + Cook Time: 30 minutes | Serving: 4

Ingredients

- 1 cup buckwheat
- 2 cups water
- 1/8 tsp salt
- 4 cups plum tomatoes, chopped
- 4 pitted green olives, sliced
- 4 pitted Kalamata olives, sliced
- 1 ½ tbsp capers, rinsed and drained
- 2 garlic cloves, minced
- 1 tbsp olive oil
- 1 tbsp chopped fresh parsley
- ¼ cup chopped fresh basil
- 1/8 tsp red chili flakes

Directions

Add buckwheat, water, and salt to a medium pot and cook covered over medium heat until tender and water absorbs, 15 to 20 minutes.

Meanwhile, in a medium bowl, mix the tomatoes, green olives, Kalamata olives, capers, garlic, olive oil, parsley, basil, and red chili flakes. Allow sitting for 5 minutes.

Serve the puttanesca with the buckwheat.

Nutritional Info per serving: Calories 387; Fat: 10g; Total Carbs: 56g; Protein: 9g

SNACKS & SIDE DISHES

Eggplant Dipped Roasted Asparagus

Prep + Cook Time: 35 minutes | Serves: 2

Ingredients

- 4 tbsp olive oil
- ½ pounds asparagus spears, trimmed
- Sea salt and black pepper to taste
- ½ tsp sweet paprika

For Eggplant Dip

- ½ pound eggplants
- 2 tsp olive oil
- ½ cup scallions, chopped
- 2 cloves garlic, minced
- 1 tbsp lemon juice
- ½ tsp chili pepper
- Salt and black pepper, to taste
- Fresh parsley, chopped for garnish

Directions

Line a parchment paper to a baking sheet. Add asparagus spears to the baking sheet. Toss with oil, sweet paprika, black pepper, and salt. Bake in the oven until cooked through for 9 minutes at 390ºF.

Add eggplants on a lined cookie sheet. Place under the broiler for about 20 minutes at 425ºF; let the eggplants to cool. Peel them and discard the stems. Place a frying pan over medium-high heat and warm olive oil. Add in garlic and onion; sauté until tender.

Using a food processor, pulse together black pepper, roasted eggplants, salt, lemon juice, scallion mixture, and chili pepper to mix evenly. Add parsley for garnishing. Serve alongside roasted asparagus spears.

Nutritional Info per serving: Calories 169; Fat: 12g; Total Carbs: 19g; Protein: 5g

Steamed Asparagus & Grilled Cauliflower Steaks

Prep + Cook Time: 20 minutes | Serves: 4

Ingredients

- 4 tbsp olive oil
- 1 head cauliflower, sliced into 'steaks'
- 1 red onion, sliced
- ¼ cup green chili sauce
- 1 tsp harissa powder
- Salt and black pepper to taste
- 1 lb asparagus, trimmed
- Juice of 1 lemon
- 1 cup water
- Fresh parsley to garnish

Directions

Preheat the grill.

In a bowl, mix the olive oil, chili sauce, and harissa. Brush the cauliflower with the mixture. Place the steaks on the grill, and cook for 6 minutes. Flip the cauliflower, grill further for 6 minutes.

Bring the water to boil over high heat, place the asparagus in a sieve, and set over the steam from the boiling water. Cook for 6 minutes. After, remove to a bowl and toss with lemon juice. Remove the grilled cauliflower to a plate; sprinkle with salt, black pepper, red onion, and parsley. Serve with the steamed asparagus.

Nutritional Info per serving: Calories 118; Fat: 9g; Total Carbs: 14g; Protein: 2g

Endive with Cheddar & Walnut Sauce

Prep + Cook Time: 15 min + cooling time | Serves: 2

Ingredients

- 1 endive heads, leaves separated
- 2 oz cheddar cheese, crumbled
- 1 cup heavy cream
- ½ tsp nutmeg
- Salt and black pepper to taste
- ½ cup toasted walnuts

Directions

In a saucepan over medium heat, warm heavy cream. Add in cheddar cheese, nutmeg, salt, and pepper and stir. Remove to a bowl and whisk with a mixer until smooth. Let cool. Arrange the endive leaves on a serving plate. Spoon the cheese mixture into the leaves and top with toasted walnuts to serve.

Nutritional Info per serving: Calories 360; Fat: 23g; Total Carbs: 15g; Protein: 12g

Asian-Style Tofu Zucchini Kabobs

Prep + Cook Time: 10 minutes | Serving: 2

Ingredients

- 8 oz extra firm tofu, pressed and cut into 1-inch cubes
- 1 medium zucchini, cut into 2-inch rounds
- 1 tbsp olive oil
- 2 tbsp freshly squeezed lemon juice
- 1 tsp smoked paprika
- 1 tsp cumin powder
- ½ tsp parsley dried
- 1 tsp garlic powder

Directions

Preheat a grill to medium heat.

Meanwhile, thread the tofu and zucchini alternately on the wooden skewers.

In a bowl, whisk the olive oil, lemon juice, paprika, parsley, cumin powder, and garlic powder. Brush the skewers all around with the mixture and place on the grill grate. Cook on both sides until golden brown, 5 minutes. Serve afterward.

Nutritional Info per serving: Calories 312; Fat: 19g; Total Carbs: 20g; Protein: 18g

Nutty Tofu Loaf

Prep + Cook Time: 65 minutes | Serving: 4

Ingredients

- 2 tbsp olive oil + extra for brushing
- 2 red onions, finely chopped
- 4 garlic cloves, minced
- 1 lb firm tofu, pressed and crumbled
- 2 tbsp soy sauce
- ¾ cup chopped walnuts
- ¼ cup buckwheat flakes
- 1 tbsp sesame seeds
- 1 cup chopped green bell peppers
- Salt and black pepper to taste
- 1 tbsp Italian seasoning
- ½ tsp brown sugar
- ½ cup tomato sauce

Directions

Preheat the oven to 350 F and grease an 8 x 4-inch loaf pan with olive oil.

Heat 1 tbsp of olive oil in a small skillet and sauté the onion and garlic until softened and fragrant, 2 minutes. Pour the onion mixture into a large bowl and mix with the tofu, soy sauce, walnuts, buckwheat flakes, sesame seeds, bell peppers, salt, black pepper, Italian seasoning, and brown sugar until well combined.

Spoon the mixture into the loaf pan, press to fit, and spread the tomato sauce on top. Bake the tofu loaf in the oven for 45 minutes to 1 hour or until well compacted.

Remove the loaf pan from the oven, invert the tofu loaf onto a chopping board, and cool for 5 minutes. Slice and serve warm.

Nutritional Info per serving: Calories 544; Fat: 39g; Total Carbs: 30g; Protein: 25g

Chili Toasted Nuts

Prep + Cook Time: 35 minutes | Serving: 4

Ingredients

- 1 cup walnuts nuts
- 1 tbsp extra-virgin olive oil, melted
- ¼ tsp hot sauce
- ¼ tsp garlic powder
- ¼ tsp onion powder

Directions

Preheat the oven to 350 F and line a baking sheet with baking paper.

In a medium bowl, mix the nuts, olive oil, hot sauce, garlic powder, and onion powder. Spread the mixture on the baking sheet and toast in the oven for 10 minutes.

Remove the sheet, allow complete cooling, and serve.

Nutritional Info per serving: Calories 267; Fat: 25g; Total Carbs: 6g; Protein: 6g

DESSERTS

Walnut & Chocolate Bars

Prep + Cook Time: 80 minutes | Serving: 4

Ingredients

- 1 cup walnuts
- 3 tbsp sunflower seeds
- 2 tbsp unsweetened chocolate chips
- 1 tbsp unsweetened cocoa powder
- 1 ½ tsp vanilla extract
- ¼ tsp cinnamon powder
- 2 tbsp melted coconut oil
- 2 tbsp toasted almond meal
- 2 tsp brown sugar

Directions

In a food processor, add the walnuts, sunflower seeds, chocolate chips, cocoa powder, vanilla extract, cinnamon powder, coconut oil, almond meal, brown sugar, and blitz a few times until coarsely combined.

Line a flat baking sheet with plastic wrap. Pour the mixture onto the sheet and place another plastic wrap on top. Use a rolling pin to flatten the batter and then remove the top plastic wrap.

Freeze the snack until firm, 1 hour. Remove from the freezer, cut into 1 ½-inch bars and enjoy immediately.

Nutritional Info per serving: Calories 302; Fat: 24g; Total Carbs: 20g; Protein: 5g

Date Cake Slices

Prep + Cook Time: 1 hour 20 minutes | Serving: 4

Ingredients

- 2 tbsp extra-virgin olive oil
- 1 tbsp flax seed powder + 3 tbsp water
- ½ cup whole-wheat flour, plus extra for dusting
- ¼ cup chopped pecans and walnuts
- 1 tsp baking powder
- 1 tsp baking soda
- 1 tsp cinnamon powder
- 1 tsp salt
- 1/3 cup water
- 1/3 cup pitted dates, chopped
- ½ cup pure date sugar
- 1 tsp vanilla extract
- ¼ cup pure date syrup for drizzling.

Directions

Preheat the oven to 350 F and lightly grease a round baking dish with some olive oil. In a small bowl, mix the flax seed powder with water and allow thickening for 5 minutes to make the flax egg.

In a food processor, add the flour, nuts, baking powder, baking soda, cinnamon powder, and salt. Blend until well combined. Add the water, dates, date sugar, and vanilla. Process until smooth with tiny pieces of dates evident.

Pour the batter into the baking dish and bake in the oven for 1 hour and 10 minutes or until a toothpick inserted comes out clean. Remove the dish from the oven, invert the cake onto a serving platter to cool, drizzle with the date syrup, slice, and serve.

Nutritional Info per serving: Calories 550; Fat: 21g; Total Carbs: 65g; Protein: 14g

Walnut Chocolate Fudge

Prep + Cook Time: 2 hours 10 minutes | Serving: 4

Ingredients

- 3 cups unsweetened chocolate chips
- ¼ cup thick coconut milk
- 1 ½ tsp vanilla extract
- A pinch salt
- 1 cup chopped walnuts

Directions

Line a 9-inch square pan with baking paper and set aside. Melt the chocolate chips, coconut milk, and vanilla in a medium pot over low heat.

Mix in the salt and nuts until well distributed and pour the mixture into the square pan. Refrigerate for at least 2 hours. Remove from the fridge, cut into squares, and serve.

Nutritional Info per serving: Calories 307; Fat: 28g; Total Carbs: 15g; Protein: 9g

Fluffy Chocolate Mousse with Strawberries

Prep + Cook Time: 30 minutes | Serves: 4

Ingredients

- 3 eggs
- ¼ tsp salt
- 8 oz dark chocolate, melted
- 1 cup heavy cream
- 1 cup fresh strawberries, sliced
- 1 vanilla extract
- 1 tbsp brown sugar

Directions

In a medium mixing bowl, whip the cream until very soft. Add the eggs, vanilla extract, and sugar; whisk to combine. Fold in the chocolate.

Divide the mousse between glasses, top with the strawberry slices, and chill in the fridge for at least 30 minutes before serving.

Nutritional Info per serving: Calories 203; Fat: 16g; Total Carbs: 17g; Protein: 6g

Chocolate & Walnut Popsicles

Prep + Cook Time: 5 minutes + 3 hours chilling | Serving: 4

Ingredients

- ½ cup unsweetened chocolate chips, melted
- 1 ½ cups oat milk
- 1 tbsp unsweetened cocoa powder
- 3 tbsp pure date syrup
- 1 tsp vanilla extract
- A handful of walnuts, chopped

Directions

In a blender, add chocolate, oat milk, cocoa powder, date syrup, vanilla, walnuts, and process until smooth. Divide the mixture into popsicle molds and freeze for 3 hours.

Dip the popsicle molds in warm water to loosen the popsicles and pull out the popsicles.

Nutritional Info per serving: Calories 315; Fat: 18g; Total Carbs: 33g; Protein: 11g

Nut Stuffed Sweet Apples

Prep + Cook Time: 35 minutes | Serving: 4

Ingredients

- 4 gala apples
- 4 tbsp almond flour
- 6 tbsp pure date sugar
- 1 cup chopped walnuts

Directions

Preheat the oven the 400 F.

Slice off the top of the apples and use a melon baller or spoon to scoop out the cores of the apples. In a bowl, mix the almond flour, date sugar, and walnuts.

Spoon the mixture into the apples and then bake in the oven for 25 minutes or until the walnuts are golden brown on top and the apples soft. Remove the apples from the oven, allow cooling, and serve.

Nutritional Info per serving: Calories 281; Fat: 12g; Total Carbs: 52g; Protein: 6g

Strawberry & Pecan Muffins

Prep + Cook Time: 35 minutes | Serves: 1

Ingredients

- 1 cup buckwheat flour
- 1 tbsp chia seeds
- ½ cup water + 3 tbsp water
- 1 ½ tsp ground cinnamon
- ½ tsp vanilla extract
- A pinch of salt
- 1 ½ tbsp coconut oil, melted
- 1 cup raspberries, mashed
- 1 tsp baking soda
- 1 tbsp apple cider vinegar
- ½ cup chopped pecans

Directions

Preheat oven to 360 F. Line a 12-hole muffin tray with parchment cups.

In a bowl, mix chia seeds with 3 tbsp of water, and let sit for 8 minutes to absorb the water. Fold in the flour, salt, cinnamon, coconut oil, mashed raspberries, and water and stir well until a homogeneous batter is formed.

Quickly stir in the baking soda and vinegar and fold in the pecans. Share the batter into the paper muffin cups with a spoon, at about two-thirds full. Bake for 22 minutes, until the centers are firm. Let cool for 5 minutes, then remove the muffins to a wire rack to cool completely.

Nutritional Info per serving: Calories 261; Fat: 16g; Total Carbs: 32g; Protein: 7g

Easy Buckwheat Chocolate Chip Cookies

Prep + Cook Time: 15 minutes | Serves: 4

Ingredients

- 1 cup ground buckwheat groats
- ½ cup coconut sugar
- ½ cup melted coconut oil
- 2 tbsp water
- 1 tsp lemon zest
- ½ tsp fine sea salt
- ½ tsp baking soda
- 1 tsp lemon juice
- ½ cup dark chocolate chips

Directions

Preheat oven to 360 F. Line a large baking tray with wax paper.

In a bowl, add the buckwheat, coconut sugar, oil, water, lemon zest, salt, and baking soda; mix well. Mix in the lemon juice, and then fold in the chocolate chips.

With a spoon, divide the dough into 12 mounds on the lined baking tray. Leave some space between the mounds. With a hand, press each ball to form cookies. Bake for 10-12 minutes at 340 F, until firm. Let cool and serve.

Nutritional Info per serving: Calories 153; Fat: 3g; Total Carbs: 6g; Protein: 12g

RECIPE INDEX

Made in the USA
Las Vegas, NV
08 February 2021